ESPECIALLY FOR

_____

FROM

_____

DATE

_____

A CELEBRATION
of the SIMPLE LIFE
Inspiring thoughts from Amish Country

Wanda E. Brunstetter

BARBOUR
PUBLISHING

Published by Barbour Publishing, Inc., P.O. Box 719, Uhrichsville, Ohio 44683, www.barbourbooks.com

Our mission is to publish and distribute inspirational products offering exceptional value and biblical encouragement to the masses.

Member of the
Evangelical Christian
Publishers Association

Printed in China.

CONTENTS

Christian Duty

INTRODUCTION

One of the things I most admire about the Amish way of life is their dedication to keeping true to their faith. While the Amish and other Plain groups would be the first to admit that they aren't perfect, their simple way of life and deep faith in God provide us with a model of how we might simplify our own lives to live better physically, emotionally, and spiritually. The Amish way of life offers us ideas on how to live a slower-paced, satisfying life with less dependence on modern things and more emphasis on God, family, and friends.

In this devotional, I've shared some of the experiences I've personally had with the Amish. These experiences have not only drawn me closer to the people I've come to know and love, but they've given me a deeper understanding and appreciation of God's amazing love. My Amish friends have inspired me to live my life a little simpler and to keep my focus on things that have eternal value.

ATTITUDE

The seed of discouragement will not grow in a thankful heart.

For the LORD seeth
not as man seeth;
for man looketh on the
outward appearance,
but the LORD looketh
on the heart.

1 Samuel 16:7

A Humble Attitude

When it comes to being humble,
Jesus set the example for us.
He went willingly to the cross,
Without resistance or making a fuss.
When others spoke of His greatness,
He withdrew to a quiet place.
A look of humility must have shone clearly
On our Savior's face.
Lord, help me to have a humble attitude,
Not prideful, conceited, or vain.
I want to be an example to others,
Never haughty, just humble and plain.

—WEB

Clothed with Humility

Yea, all of you be subject one to another,
and be clothed with humility:
for God resisteth the proud,
and giveth grace to the humble.

1 Peter 5:5

During one of our trips to Ohio, my husband and I met with Dr. Elton Lehman, who gave us a tour of the birthing center in Mt. Eaton, which he started several years ago. I was impressed with the facilities but even more so with Dr. Lehman's humility and caring attitude. Even though he's no longer working full-time at the clinic, he fills in when needed. His love and concern for the Amish people were the reasons for starting the birthing center. His humility was evident as he spoke of his desire to make a place where Amish women could have their babies in a safe environment that reminded them of home.

The Amish culture is embedded in the German word *Gellassenheit*, which means yielding to a higher authority and becoming a humble person. The Bible teaches us to be clothed with humility. That means we are to wear it all the time so that others may see Christ living in us. Humility isn't just about not bragging; it's about being willing to do the most menial tasks. It's about serving others and thereby serving the Lord, without needing any recognition. The humility I saw in Dr. Lehman reminds me of the gentle, humble spirit I've seen in so many of our Amish friends. It encourages me to wear the clothes of humility, too.

Heavenly Father,
remind me often to wear the clothes of humility.
May others see You living in me. Amen.

Attitude of Acceptance

It's not easy to accept some things;
We often worry, grumble, and fret.
How much better it would be
If we trusted God instead of getting upset.
An attitude of acceptance
Gives one a sense of peace.
When we trust God to know what's best for us,
Our anxiety and tension will cease.

—WEB

Accept What You Must

Casting all your care upon him; for he careth for you.
1 Peter 5:7

If there's one thing I've learned about the Amish, it's their ability to accept things that happen to them as God's will. An Amish couple we know are unable to have children of their own. As much as they would like to be parents, they've accepted it as God's will. Rather than brooding about their situation, they take pleasure in spending time with their nieces and nephews and ministering to others in need.

Another Amish man we know is confined to a wheelchair due to a childhood accident. While some might question God and bemoan their situation, he chooses to remain positive and does whatever he can.

Life isn't always fair, but if we learn to appreciate what we have and trust God with our future, we'll feel a sense of peace and acceptance. Remember this week to accept what you must and change what you can. Look to the future with a sense of hope and thank God for each new day, for we really do have much to be grateful for.

Heavenly Father,
there are many things in my life
over which I have no control.
Help me learn to accept those things,
knowing that You are in control.
Fill me with Your perfect peace,
and give me a heart of acceptance. Amen.

Joyful Attitude

Birds are joyful every day,
Just like children out at play.
Their sweet, shrill singing is the way we know
That the birds are happy, and they let it show.
It's good to be cheerful and wear a smile,
Thanking God and giving praises all the while.
The Bible tells us to rejoice and be glad,
Just like the birds, we're to be joyful, not sad.

—WEB

Joyful Hearts

This is the day which the LORD hath made;
we will rejoice and be glad in it.

PSALM 118:24

Every time my husband and I have been invited into an Amish home for supper, we've enjoyed the light banter, joke telling, and laughter that accompanied the meal. During such an occasion, one of our Amish friends volunteered to play the part of my ventriloquist dummy as I put on a short routine. Everyone had a good laugh over that.

Having grown up in a house where laughter was scarce, I find it refreshing to be with people who like to laugh and have a good time. In fact, I often look for things to laugh about, knowing that laughter is not only good for me emotionally, but physically as well.

There are times when I might not feel like laughing, but if I remind myself to look around, there's always something to smile about—a frisky pet, singing birds, flowers in bloom, children at play.

The Bible tells us in Proverbs 17:22 that a merry heart is good medicine. Just like the birds that sing in my yard, our Amish friends know how to share their joy with others. Make a list of some things that bring a smile to your face. Remember that a joyful heart is pleasing to the Lord, and it's an added benefit to know that it's good for you, too.

Heavenly Father,
remind me to look at the brighter side of life.
Thank You for the gift of laughter.
Help me to use if often. Amen.

Attitude of Forgiveness

An attitude of forgiveness doesn't always come easy;
It's our human nature to carry a grudge or retaliate.
But God's Word says that to be forgiven,
we must forgive;
Jesus taught that we're to love others, not hate.
With heartfelt forgiveness comes healing,
And to be forgiven we must first forgive.
It will draw us closer to God in our Christian walk,
Through the things we say and the way we live.

—WEB

True Forgiveness

For if ye forgive men their trespasses,
your heavenly Father will also forgive you.
Matthew 6:14

On October 2, 2006, a terrible tragedy that shocked the world occurred in a small Pennsylvania Amish community. An English man, who lived and worked in the area, entered an Amish school-house and shot ten girls before turning the gun on himself. Five of the girls were killed and five were seriously injured. Everyone in the community, the children's families most of all, were stunned and deeply wounded by this senseless, unbelievable act. Instead of anger and retribution, however, the families of the dead and injured chose to forgive the man who had done the evil deed. A few days after the attack, I was asked by a reporter if it was true that the Amish would really forgive the shooter, and if so, how could that be? I replied, "It is true that the Amish will forgive the man, but this kind of forgiveness comes only from God."

The Amish community not only forgave the shooter, but they raised money to help the man's wife and children through the ordeal. As surprising as it might have seemed to the world, half of the mourners at the gunman's funeral were Amish. The Amish knew they had a choice to make. They could either harbor resentment or choose to forgive. They knew that without forgiveness, their hearts would never heal.

Is there someone you need to forgive? Is there something you need to seek forgiveness for? Why not do that today?

Heavenly Father,
forgive me if I have wronged someone,
and help me to find forgiveness in my heart toward
anyone who has done wrong to me. Amen.

Patient Attitude

❧

The nature of a flower is to wait patiently for spring.

Flowers don't worry or complain about every little thing.

The nature of a flower is an example to all.

When wind and rain threaten,

a flower stands straight and tall.

Let the flowers be your example for having a patient attitude.

For when you face each day with patience,

you'll be in a better mood.

—WEB

Patience Pays Off

I waited patiently for the LORD;
and he inclined unto me, and heard my cry.

PSALM 40:1

During one of our visits to an Amish schoolhouse in Indiana, my husband made some balloon animals for the children. Since Richard has been blowing up balloons for a good many years, his lungs are strong and he rarely uses a pump. The children were impressed at how easy he made it look, and several of the boys wanted to try blowing up a balloon. After a few attempts, all except one of the red-faced boys gave up. The determined boy had a bit more patience than the others. He continued trying to blow up the balloon until he ran out of air and passed out for a few seconds. Undaunted and unhurt, he picked himself up and continued blowing until his balloon was fully inflated.

Seeing the determination of this young boy made me think of how easily some people give up when they're faced with a challenge. Sometimes we give up praying because we don't receive an answer quickly enough. God wants us to wait patiently for Him, and He wants us to pray and continually seek to do His will.

Are you faced with a challenge today that seems daunting? Ask the Lord for the courage and strength to keep going. Ask Him for an attitude of patience as you wait for answers from Him.

Heavenly Father,
sometimes when I'm feeling stressed or in a hurry,
I run out of patience. Help me remember in
such times to take a deep breath, say a prayer,
and wait patiently for answers. Amen.

Attitude of Contentment

The birds of the air don't worry or fret;
They don't complain when it rains and they get wet.
The birds of the air sing a sweet melody;
Their simple contentment is really the key.
Our Father cares for the birds of the air,
And He cares for us when we offer a prayer.
He provides for the birds with insects and seeds;
He provides for His children's daily needs.
There's much we can learn from the birds of the air,
Who don't worry about what they're going to wear.
If we learn to be content like the birds of the air,
Our life will be blessed with His tender care.

—WEB

Lasting Contentment

Not that I speak in respect of want:
for I have learned, in whatsoever state I am,
therewith to be content.

PHILIPPIANS 4:11

The last time my husband and I stayed with our Amish friends in Pennsylvania, I observed their grandchildren playing together. They weren't bored and didn't complain because there was nothing to do. They found enjoyment in simple things like reading, playing a ball game, petting their dog, riding their scooters, swinging, and swimming in the pond. They didn't need computers or electronic games. They laughed and talked together and didn't send text messages in order to communicate.

In our fast-paced electronic age, many "Englishers" don't take the time to enjoy the simple things life has to offer. We rush from place to place, hurry to complete our tasks, and find that our lives are full of stress and worry. We've become exhausted and discontented because we don't spend enough quality time with our family and friends. Many people strive so hard to get ahead that they don't see what's right beside them. Material things don't bring true happiness, nor do they bring lasting contentment. When we look around at the beauty God created and find joy in being with those we love, our discontent fades and appreciation sets in.

Heavenly Father,
remind me to appreciate the things You've given me;
and no matter what's going on in the world around me,
help me to learn to be content in whatever state I'm in.
Amen.

Attitude of Trust

When you're discouraged
And feeling a bit down,
Answers for your troubles
Are waiting to be found.
Put your trust in God;
He'll show you the way.
God watches over you
At night and through the day.
An attitude of trust
Is what every Christian needs.
Trust God fully and follow
Wherever He leads.

—WEB

Complete Trust

*I will say of the LORD, He is my refuge and my fortress:
my God; in him will I trust.*

PSALM 91:2

The Amish are some of the most trusting people I know. They trust their horses to pull their buggies. They trust their older children to care for the younger ones. They trust God to provide for all of their needs.

When my husband and I visited an Amish schoolhouse for the first time, even though the teachers had never met us, they trusted us to come in peace. In fact, we were welcomed into their classroom.

God wants us to trust Him in all things. He is our fortress, our shelter in the time of storm. Are you able to lay your worries and cares aside and trust that the Lord will see you through anything life throws at you? In Numbers 6:25, we are told that the Lord makes His face shine upon us. Knowing that God is always with us and that His face is actually shining on us should give a sense of security and trust, even in the most frightening circumstances. A calm mind and a confident heart are available to every believer. Ask God to teach you to trust Him more and help you to relax in Him.

*Heavenly Father,
when my world seems to be crashing in,
I feel frightened and insecure.
Give me a gentle reminder that
I need to put my trust in You
and not focus on my circumstances.
Give me a calm mind and confident heart.
Teach me to trust You more. Amen.*

Positive Attitude

As I search for something positive to think about,
My mind is sometimes filled with doubt.
There are so many negative things around,
Yet I know there are good things to be found.
So as I look up at the sky tonight,
I notice across the horizon, clouds so bright,
With streaks of red and a hazy pink hue,
The sky is a brilliant dark blue.
As I gaze upon this glorious sight,
I know the Great Artist has done it right.
God painted the sky for all to behold
So that His glory could surely be told.
There's always something positive to be found,
For the miracles of God's handiwork abound.

—WEB

Think on These Things

Finally, brethren, whatsoever things are true, whatsoever things are honest, whatsoever things are just, whatsoever things are pure, whatsoever things are lovely, whatsoever things are of good report, if there be any virtue, and if there be any praise, think on these things.

PHILIPPIANS 4:8

With all of the negative things going on in our world, it's easy to become depressed and allow our minds to be filled with negative thoughts. However, the Bible clearly states in Philippians 4:8 that we are to think on positive things.

One thing that became clear to me when we began making friends with the Amish was their positive outlook on life. Not only do our Amish friends enjoy telling jokes and sharing stories, but they like to focus on the beauty of God's creation. I've noticed that most Amish gardens are abundant with colorful flowers. Birdhouses and feeders can also be found in their yards. Observing the beauty of flowers and watching the birds at the feeders is not only enjoyable, but it fills our minds with positive thoughts.

To be happy and to keep from having negative thoughts, we must focus on the positive things around us. Flowers, trees, birds, sunsets, and newborn babies are just a few of the things that bring me joy and fill my mind with positive thoughts.

If we don't think positive thoughts, we can easily become negative, cynical, and depressed. Take a few moments to write down several things you appreciate about your surroundings. Make a list of things that are true, honest, just, pure, lovely, and of good report. When you do, your heart will feel a little lighter and your outlook will be a little brighter.

Heavenly Father,
when my mind becomes filled with negative thoughts,
remind me that Your Word tells me to think on
positive things. Amen.

Thankful Attitude

We should be thankful for the abundance that is ours,
For the beauty of this world, the sun, moon, and stars.
For our family, friends, and God's everlasting love,
We should give thanks to the Father above.
We should be thankful for the clothes we wear
And for the opportunities we have to share.
For the Son whom God sent because of His love,
We should offer our thanks to the Father above.

—WEB

Giving Thanks

Oh, give thanks unto the LORD, for he is good:
for his mercy endureth for ever.

PSALM 136:1

The Amish we know seem to appreciate all that they have. On more than one occasion, I have given some of the books I've written to our Amish friends' children and grandchildren. Each time the children have said thank you without having to be told to do so by their parents. Perhaps that is because they have been taught at an early age to say thank you when they receive a gift or someone has done something kind for them.

While it's important to tell others when we are thankful for something they've done, it's even more important to tell God thank You for all that He's given us—our homes, jobs, family, friends, and the beauty of His creation. Despite the unpleasant things that go on around us, every believer should have a heart of thankfulness. Knowing that God can use all things for His good is more than enough reason for us to give thanks in everything. Do you want to please God and get to know Him better? Then remember to tell Him thank You every time you pray.

Heavenly Father,
when others do nice things for me,
help me remember to say thank you.
And when I pray, help me remember to thank You
in advance for all that You do. Amen.

Loving Attitude

Let no bad thoughts toward anyone stay in your mind.
Observe the Golden Rule and to others be kind.
Vow to treat those you meet as you want them to treat you.
Emphasize a caring attitude in all that you do.

Offer to do a favor for someone you know,
Thinking about others, your love will show.
Helping someone who has a need,
Every chance you get, do a good deed.
Reaching out to people with a heartfelt prayer,
Sharing of yourself lets them know you care.

—WEB

Love beyond Measure

If we love one another, God dwelleth in us,
and his love is perfected in us.

1 JOHN 4:12

People who set aside selfish ambition and seek the good of others have an attitude that pleases God. I recently saw this selfless attitude when my husband and I visited one of our Amish friends in Kentucky. The wife, pretty much bedridden due to a stroke, was being lovingly cared for by her husband of many years. It touched my heart when he set up folding chairs for us in his wife's bedroom so that she could be included in our conversation. I saw a look of commitment on the man's face, which was a sure sign of his love and dedication. Ephesians 5:25 says, "Husbands, love your wives, even as Christ also loved the church, and gave himself for it."

Another one of our Amish friends used to be English. She loved her husband so much that she gave up her modern way of life to become part of his Amish faith. Ephesians 5:22 reminds us: "Wives submit yourselves unto your own husband, as unto the Lord."

God's Word commands us to love one another and to love Him with our heart, soul, and mind. Imagine how different our world would be if everyone loved God and their fellow humans. Think of something special you can do for someone you love, and ask God to help you love the unlovely.

Heavenly Father,
Thank You for loving me so much that You sent
Your Son to die on the cross for my sins.
I want to show love toward others
so that they will see You living in me. Amen.

RESPONSIBILITY

The most satisfying thing in life is to have been able to give a large part of one's self to others.

Let us hear the conclusion
of the whole matter:
Fear God, and keep his
commandments:
for this is the whole
duty of man.

ECCLESIASTES 12:13

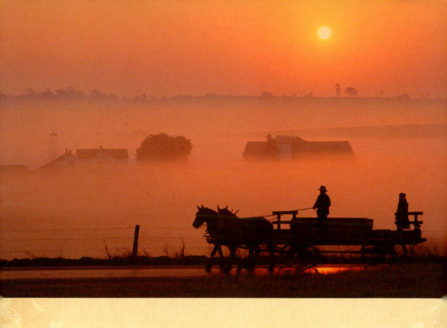

Responsibility to Worship

Church is the place we go to listen and pray;

It's where we learn about God and how to obey.

Church is the place we go to sing songs of praise;

It's where we worship and learn of God's amazing ways.

Church is where we gather with family and friends;

It's a place of repentance, where broken hearts mend.

It's our responsibility to worship the Lord;

Gathering with other believers should never be ignored.

—WEB

True Worship

But the hour cometh, and now is,
when the true worshippers shall
worship the Father in spirit and in truth:
for the Father seeketh such to worship him.

JOHN 4:23

The Amish families we know believe in togetherness. They eat together, work together, play together, pray together, and attend church together.

My husband and I attended an Amish church service with some of our Amish friends one Sunday last summer, arriving by horse and buggy. Even though we couldn't understand all of the German words that were spoken, we felt a true sense of worship in the songs that were sung and in the ministers' messages. We sensed the people's devotion to God and felt welcomed in their worship service.

One of our responsibilities as Christians is to worship God, as well as to make any visitors in our congregation feel welcome. We don't have to be in church to worship Him, however. We can worship God every day through prayer, Bible reading, and meditation. True worship requires all of our heart, soul, mind, and strength. If you worship God with your whole heart this week, you will be lifted up and will feel His presence. When you attend church this Sunday with your friends and family, concentrate fully on God, and ask Him to give you a worshipful heart.

Heavenly Father,
When I worship You with my whole heart
I feel myself being drawn closer to You.
Thank You for who You are and for all that You do.
May I sense Your presence
as I worship You this week. Amen.

Responsibility to Work

Hanging out the wash to dry,

Another chore; I seem to sigh.

The responsibility of doing my work

Is something I know I cannot shirk.

And when I smell the sweet perfume

Of sun-washed clothes, it ends my gloom.

For the fresh scent reminds me of God's love

As He looks down from heaven above.

My sins were once dirty, just like the clothes,

But Jesus washed them away when He died and rose.

So as I continue to do my chores—

Cleaning the cupboards, scrubbing the floors—

I'll remind myself that my true reward

Is knowing that I'm working for the Lord.

—WEB

Whatever You Do

And whatsoever ye do, do it heartily,
as to the Lord, and not unto men.

COLOSSIANS 3:23

I've had the privilege of helping some of our Amish friends do a few of their chores—washing dishes, baking homemade bread, setting and clearing the table. Never once did I hear anyone complain about the work she or he had to do. In fact, it was done without question.

There's something satisfying and rewarding about work, and tasks can actually be enjoyable if we have someone to visit with while we're doing them. Even tasks done alone can be satisfying. The smell of laundry that has been hung on the line to dry outdoors brings a sense of satisfaction. Cleaning windows, scrubbing floors, and doing the dishes should be looked upon with gratification, knowing you've done your best.

Among the Amish, work is viewed as helping others. They work cooperatively within the family, and even young children are included when they're given simple chores to do. Maybe the reason my Amish friends don't complain about the work they're required to do is because they've learned that whatever they do, they're doing it as unto the Lord and not unto men.

Whatever work you're required to do this week, it will seem easier if you determine to do it for the Lord.

Heavenly Father,
As I go about my work this week,
help me remember to do all my chores
as if I'm doing them for You. Amen.

Responsibility to Fellowship

❦

Where two or three are gathered,
Fellowship is found.
The hum of gentle voices
Is such a pleasant sound.
Time spent with others
Is always a special treat.
Solitude can be lonely,
But fellowship is sweet.

—WEB

Where Two Are Gathered

For where two or three are gathered together in
my name, there am I in the midst of them.
MATTHEW 18:20

A few years ago, my husband and I were in Ohio, where I was scheduled to do some book signings. We were pleased when a couple of our Amish friends from Pennsylvania hired a driver to bring them to Ohio so we could spend a few days together. Even though our time was short, the fellowship we had was sweet. We did some shopping, shared a few meals, and attended church together. We told stories from the past, talked about the future, and exchanged prayer requests. Even though our Amish friends dress differently than we do and live a different lifestyle, we have become close and enjoy each other's company. We consider this couple to be two of our dearest friends and look forward to our times of fellowship with them.

God doesn't want us to close ourselves off from others. He wants us to spend time with other believers and gather in His name. I always feel the presence of God when I'm with a dear Christian friend. When we share our joys, sorrows, and prayer requests with others, we feel comforted and not alone.

Do you know of someone who is lonely or needs a friend? Why not find some time to fellowship with that person this week? You'll both feel blessed if you do.

Heavenly Father,
whenever I feel lonely and I hear from a friend,
I always feel blessed and uplifted.
Help me to become sensitive to the needs of my friends
who may need to be uplifted, too. Amen.

Responsibility to Family

No one can take the place of my family;
They mean the world to me.
Husband, son, daughter, and grandchildren,
My love for family will always be.
There's nothing quite so special
As spending time with those I love.
I'm sure God is pleased
As He looks down from above.
When I spend time with family,
I get to know them more.
I share with them, they share with me;
It's like an open door.
So I'll make a note to remind myself
That a solitary life is not for me.
I'm sure it pleases God
To hear us say, "You. . .me. . .we."

—WEB

Family Ties

Children's children are the crown of old men;
and the glory of children are their fathers.

PROVERBS 17:6

My husband and I had the privilege of staying with some of our Amish friends for nearly a week last summer. While we were with them, we observed the relationship they have with their family members. We saw a special closeness and deep respect between parents and children, grandparents and grandchildren, aunts, uncles, nieces, nephews, and cousins. Our Amish friends' grandchildren love them so much that they even wanted to help build their new house. I believe this kind of love and respect is something every family could have if they read God's Word and follow His teachings. How sad that some people treat strangers better than they do their own family members. Our first priority should be to love and serve God. Our second priority should be to love and serve our families.

Biblical parenting is no guarantee of having godly children, but we should cultivate a spiritual interest in our children and grandchildren. The richest legacy we can leave our children is a Christian example. Is there something special you can do for a family member today? When was the last time you told someone in your family how much you love and appreciate them? Why not do that today?

Heavenly Father,
thank You for my family,
whom I love and appreciate so much.
Help me remember to tell them
often that I love them. Amen.

Responsibility to Friends

The gift of friendship means so much,

It's always good to stay in touch.

With a dear friend you can laugh and cry,

Knowing they won't judge or ask you why.

A friend is someone who gives and accepts advice;

There's no greater gift than a friend for life.

A friend sticks closer than a brother, we're told.

The gift of friendship is worth more than gold.

—WEB

A True Friend

A friend loveth at all times.
PROVERBS 17:17

During a visit to Ohio, one of our Amish friends told us about a surprise anniversary party he and his wife had planned for some of their friends. As they gave us the details about the great lengths they'd gone to in order to keep the anniversary couple from finding out about the party, I was struck with the realization that true friends go the extra mile to do something special for someone they care about.

Another instance of friendship came to mind during the time we spent with some of our Amish friends in Pennsylvania. They actually gave up their bed and moved to the basement so we could have a room on the main floor.

Another time, some of our Amish friends in Indiana invited me to do a book signing in their home, and they invited their friends and relatives to come and meet me. We had an enjoyable evening as I signed books, visited, and ate refreshments.

The depth of friendship isn't merely about spending time together or doing the right thing toward our friends. It's about sacrifice and doing for others as we would have done to us. It's about showing friends that we love them just as Christ loves us. Is there something special you can do for one of your friends today?

Heavenly Father,
help me to be sensitive to my friends' needs,
and remind me of the responsibility
I have to cultivate the relationship
I have with them.
May each of my friends feel
Your love today. Amen.

Responsibility to Our Neighbors

"Love your neighbor as yourself,"
The Bible says to do.
If we truly love ourselves,
Then we'll love our neighbors, too.

—WEB

The Neighborly Thing

Thou shalt love thy neighbour as thyself.
ROMANS 13:9

Traveling down the road in our rented car, I was surprised to see an elderly Amish woman struggling to get her horse out of a ditch and back on the road. Before my husband had a chance to respond to the situation, our Amish friend who sat in the backseat shouted, "Please, stop the car; I need to help that woman!" My husband had barely stopped the car when our friend jumped out and raced over to the horse and buggy. Having grown up around horses, she wasn't afraid, and quickly had the horse under control so the elderly woman could get back in her buggy. Watching the situation unfold, I thought of the Bible verse that reminds us that we are to love our neighbors as ourselves. That means helping when we see a need.

It's easy to find a reason not to get involved—indifference, busyness, or fear. Life for the Amish isn't about seeing if they can get ahead of their neighbors, but seeing if they can help their neighbors.

As we seek to follow the Lord, we should look for opportunities to help our neighbors. We may be the only Jesus they'll ever see. Is there something you might do to help one of your neighbors this week?

Heavenly Father,
sometimes I become so caught up with the
busyness of life that I forget about my neighbors.
Show me some ways that I might reach out to
one of my neighbors this week. Amen.

Responsibility to Strengthen Our Faith

God made the butterfly in a special way,
A fuzzy little caterpillar builds a cocoon one day.
All cozy and secure the tiny creature sleeps,
It makes no sound, not even a peep.
Then one day when the timing is right,
The world is rewarded with a wonderful sight.
That little caterpillar, once fuzzy and long,
Flies out of its home with wings so strong.
It has suddenly become a beautiful butterfly.
Flying free it sails up to the sky,
God made this insect in a special way,
A tiny miracle, wouldn't you say?
Flowers that have died come back in the spring;
Robins return to twitter and sing.
If we look for miracles that are all around,
It will strengthen our faith in ways that astound.

—WEB

Faith That Pleases God

But without faith it is impossible to please him:
for he that cometh to God must believe that he is,
and that he is a rewarder of them that diligently seek him.

HEBREWS 11:6

When several of the RV factories in the northeastern part of Indiana closed down or cut back on their operations, many of our Amish friends found themselves out of a job. Yet despite this setback, our friends' faith remained strong. They told us that they knew God would provide and show them how to find a way to support their families.

We have a responsibility to strengthen our faith, but due to the trials we face, our faith sometimes wavers. Faith is simply believing that what God says, He will do. It's easy for our faith to waver during trying times, but just like muscles in the body, we must exercise our faith. We can help our faith move higher by praying often. We can help our faith grow stronger by reading God's Word. We can renew our faith by claiming His promises. We tend to drift spiritually if we take our eyes off the Lord. If you're beginning to drift, remember, you'll stay close to Him by reading His Word every day and praying often. It's the only way to really strengthen your faith.

Remember this week that God is always with you and will never leave. If you continue to trust and follow Him, even when things seem hopeless, your faith will be strengthened.

Heavenly Father,
during times of trouble my faith sometimes wavers.
Remind me through Your Word that You are always with me.
Knowing that is enough to strengthen my faith. Amen.

Responsibility to Maintain Simplicity

❧

Maintaining a life of simplicity
Is what the Amish culture is about.
We could learn a lot from the Amish,
There's really no doubt.
Spending time with others
And helping when there's a need,
Focusing on God and following Him
With every word and deed.
Acquiring things and getting ahead
Is the focus for many these days.
But maintaining a life of simplicity
Can be accomplished in numerous ways.

—WEB

Simplify

Teach me thy way, O Lord,
and lead me in a plain path.

PSALM 27:11

I love spending time with our Amish friends' children and grandchildren. I find it refreshing to watch them at play. I also enjoy watching Amish parents and grandparents visiting and working with one another. Their simple dress and simple way of doing things awakens a desire within me to simplify my life.

I've noticed with a sense of sadness that many of us "Englishers" are so immersed in TV, computers, cell phones, and other electronic gadgets that we barely know how to communicate with each other anymore. Even when we do visit, the drone of the TV or radio is often in the background. Is it any wonder that so many people feel uptight and stressed out?

We can always find ways to simplify our lives if we just eliminate some of the unnecessary things. Consider some of the things that make up your day and ask yourself, "Is this really necessary?" The Amish way of life reminds us that there is satisfaction and joy in simplicity. God never intended our lives to be so complicated. This week, carefully examine how you spend your time. What are some ways you can simplify?

Heavenly Father,
when I get caught up in "things,"
help me to redirect my focus.
Lead me in a plain, simple path that focuses
on You and not on things. Amen.

Responsibility to Rest

I look up at the sky, watching the clouds overhead.
Rather than working, I'll think of God instead.
Watching the sun come up and watching it go down,
Walking on the beach to see the waves pound.
Playing with my grandchildren as we laugh and talk,
Cuddling a kitten or taking a walk.
Going with a friend to visit the zoo,
Feeding the birds in my yard, for God created them, too.
I need to relax and have a responsibility to rest,
For God loves me, and He knows what's best.

—WEB

A Time to Rest

And he said unto them,
Come ye yourselves apart into a desert place, and rest a while.
MARK 6:31

When my husband and I spent a week with some of our Amish friends last summer, I had to give up my computer, TV, hair dryer, and curling iron, because electricity was not readily available. I didn't mind giving up TV, because I don't watch it much anyhow. Thanks to a fresh perm, my hair looked okay. Even though I missed my computer, it was kind of nice to take a break from answering e-mail messages. So what did I do all week besides visiting with our Amish friends and helping out wherever I could? I rested and reflected on the beauty of God's creation and focused on His goodness to us.

It's important to examine ourselves spiritually through rest and reflection. We can't do our best work with nerves that are taut from being constantly under pressure. It's not good to spend all our time working and pushing to get ahead. Jesus invited His disciples to come with Him to a quiet place where they could be refreshed.

Mediation and time spent with the Lord gives us more understanding and a sense of oneness with Him. It helps us refresh and renew, both physically and mentally. We can draw closer to God when we rest and meditate on Him. If we think about God's Word, we'll gain strength and renewal. Why not look for a quiet place today where you can rest and find a sense of strength in Jesus?

Heavenly Father,
Sometimes I get caught up in my work
and forget that I need to rest.
Remind me regularly that I need to rest in You. Amen.

Responsibility to Learn

Though I once had an earthly father whom I called my own,
I'm so glad I have a heavenly Father,
sitting on His kingly throne.
He loves me and guides me all along the way;
He teaches and instructs me each and every day.
Despite my busy schedule, I have a responsibility to learn;
When I spend time with God, I learn from Him in turn.
I'm glad He is my Father, and I, His child in need;
I'm thankful that He guides me in every word and deed.

—WEB

A Good Education

If any of you lack wisdom, let him ask of God,
that giveth to all men liberally, and upbraideth not;
and it shall be given him.

JAMES 1:5

My husband and I have had the privilege of visiting several Amish schoolhouses, and we've spoken to many Amish schoolteachers about the scholars they teach. One of the things I noticed as I sat at the back of a schoolhouse and observed the children one day was how well-behaved and attentive they were. To some it might seem strange that the Amish are only schooled until they graduate from the eighth grade, but they're taught very well. From my observation, an eighth-grade education among the Amish is equal to a twelfth-grade education in our English schools.

It's important for everyone to have a well-rounded education and sit under good teachers who want their students to learn. It's equally important for us to have spiritual wisdom and the ability to discern the will of God in our lives. This kind of wisdom doesn't come from a formal education, although scriptures are read in the Amish schoolhouse, and the Lord's Prayer is said every day. The kind of spiritual wisdom each of us needs is given by God, through spending time with Him in prayer and meditation. As we are told in James 1:5, if we lack wisdom in spiritual matters, all we have to do is ask God and He'll give it to us without reproach.

Heavenly Father,
grant me wisdom to know Your will for my life,
and remind me to teach my children and grandchildren
to seek after Your wisdom, too. Amen.

Responsibility to Be Obedient

The moon and sun obey God's will,
And we should do the same.
To listen to His still, small voice
Should be every believer's aim.
When we get off track and disobey,
We'll feel it in our soul.
Being obedient to God's commands
Should always be our goal.

—WEB

Trained to Pull

For as by one man's disobedience many were made sinners,
so by the obedience of one shall many be made righteous.
ROMANS 5:19

Most of the horses we've seen in Amish country are well-behaved and cooperate with their owners. The reason for this is because they're trained to be obedient so they can safely pull their owner's buggy. One of our Amish friends trains buggy horses. When I spoke with him about his job, he told me that if a horse isn't thoroughly trained, it won't obey the proper commands and could prove to be dangerous on the road. An untrained horse will pull against the reins, going in whatever direction it chooses. An untrained horse might become distracted by things going on around him and become spooked.

Just as a horse must learn obedience to its master, we must learn obedience to God and open ourselves up to His will for our lives. If we don't listen to His voice and obey His commandments, we'll end up going in the wrong direction. We'll be like a disobedient horse, pulling against the reins and getting ourselves into all kinds of trouble. How much better off we'd be if we learned to listen to God's voice instead of trying to do things our own way.

Heavenly Father,
I want to do Your will.
Mold me and make me into the kind
of person You wish me to be.
Guide me and direct me so that the things
I do are pleasing in Your sight. Amen.

Responsibility to Set a Good Example

Setting a good example for others to see,

Caring about them and not always me.

If we let our light shine by doing good deeds,

The gospel will be spread with the sowing of seeds.

—WEB

Letting Our Lights Shine

Let your light so shine before men,
that they may see your good works
and glorify your Father which is in heaven.

MATTHEW 5:16

Every year I receive hundreds of letters and e-mail messages from readers who say they've been influenced in some way by the stories in my books depicting the Amish way of life. In our modern world, where too much emphasis is placed on material things, many people are searching for something that will offer them a slower pace and help them focus on the important things in life. The Amish and other Plain People have set an example for that, which is why I believe so many people are fascinated with and drawn to their way of life.

Just as the Amish have given us an example for living more simply, every Christian should set an example to the world, showing others a godly way of life. Letting our light shine so that the world may see our good works will bring glory to God. Remember as you go about your day that you may be the only Jesus some of your friends, neighbors, and family will ever see. What we say and what we do is how we show others that Christ lives in us. We should all want to make a difference in other people's lives. Make a list of some ways that you might set an example for Christianity today.

Heavenly Father,
help me remember in all that I say and do
to set an example for others so that they will see
You living in me and come to know You, too. Amen.

Responsibility to Seek Inner Peace

Looking out my window on a winter's afternoon

To catch a glimpse of wonder that will be gone too soon.

Seeing the snowdrifts for miles around

Covering the trees in their winter gowns.

Icicles hang so precariously still

As they glimmer across each windowsill.

The sun casts a shadow as it ducks behind a cloud;

A branch with a blanket of snow has bowed.

I'm reminded that God made the snow, falling like fleece,

I, along with the wintry world, feel a sense of peace.

—WEB

Perfect Peace

Thou wilt keep him in perfect peace,
whose mind is stayed on thee: because he trusteth in thee.
Isaiah 26:3

I always feel a sense of peace when I'm visiting one of our Amish friend's homes. Some people may believe that the Amish are peaceful because they live close to the land—surrounded by farm animals, growing crops, flowers, and trees. However, I believe that the Amish feel a sense of peace because of their sincere faith in God.

Life can be difficult at times, but nothing can separate us from God's love. God gives all believers a sense of peace if they keep their eyes on Him and not on the things of this world. It's comforting to know that God keeps the earth rotating and the seasons changing. He makes the sun rise every morning and sets the sun at just the right time each evening. All that God does should remind us that He is in control, which will give us a perfect peace. When you go to bed tonight, you can relax in the knowledge that God is in control and sleep in peace. Make a list of the things that give you a sense of peace. How are they related to your relationship to God?

Heavenly Father,
when I have a peaceful attitude, it's so much easier to cope.
May Your perfect peace, which passes all understanding,
fill my soul today. Amen.

Responsible for the Words we Speak

Saying kind words is what we should do.

It pleases God and makes friends, too.

Complaining isn't pleasant to anyone who hears;

A soft answer is pleasing to everyone's ears.

So let's use lots of kindness in everything we say;

Follow God's example, and don't forget to pray.

Saying kind words is what we should do.

It pleases God and makes friends, too.

—WEB

What We Say

Pleasant words are as an honeycomb,
sweet to the soul, and health to the bones.

PROVERBS 16:24

During one of our visits to an Amish schoolhouse in Indiana, I did a short routine with my ventriloquist puppet, Grandma Yoder. The children were very taken with the puppet, and afterward I was flooded with questions. "Where was that puppet's voice coming from?" one student asked. "Did you have a tape recorder hidden somewhere?" Another student was sure that my husband must have been speaking for the puppet. I explained to the children that I'm a ventriloquist, and the voice they heard for the puppet was actually me, and that I'm able to speak without moving my lips. I was then plied with even more questions. So I gave a short demonstration, carrying on further conversation with my puppet and explaining about the substitutions I use in order to make certain letters in the alphabet sound like other letters that can be said without lip movement.

Thinking about sound substitutions and how easily they can be misunderstood reminds me of the words we say to others and how sometimes what we say can be misconstrued. A slight exaggeration, repeating something we've heard, or spreading rumors about someone else can all lead to misunderstandings. God cautions us in His Word to be careful what we say. We are reminded in Psalm 19:3 that there is no speech or language where our voice is not heard.

Heavenly Father,
help me remember to think before I speak,
and always to substitute a kind word for something
that will hurt or confuse another. Amen.

Responsibility to Be Committed

*Commitment means dedication
To something you know you should do.
Commitment in every aspect of our lives
Is what God wishes we all knew.
Commitment to God and others
Is part of the Christian way.
Commitment to worshipping Him
Each and every day.*

—WEB

Becoming Committed

And let us not be weary in well doing:
for in due season we shall reap, if we faint not.

Our Amish friends are some of the most dedicated people I know. They are committed to God by their regular church attendance and living a life that stresses humility and caring for others. They're loyal to family, friends, and neighbors. They're devoted to preserving their way of life.

The life of commitment, for anyone, Amish or English, means being steadfast. We're committed to things we know are helpful to someone. We're dedicated to the things we realize are important. We're faithful to do things that our parents and teachers require of us. If we are first committed to God, then we're more likely to be faithful to other things as well. Even if we weren't taught by our parents to be committed, we can teach ourselves.

Think of one thing this week that you'd like to improve about your life, and then ask God to help you stay committed to it. Set aside a regular time to read your Bible and pray. If you do this every day, it will strengthen your faith and help you stay committed to serving God.

Heavenly Father,
I want to remain firmly committed to You.
Show me some ways to improve my life
as a Christian so that others
will be committed to You, too. Amen.

Responsibility to Remember our Roots

It's good to look to the future
And not always live in the past.
But there's a time to reflect on memories
With deep meaning that will last.
There are those who've lived before us,
Who, by their example, showed Christian love.
There are those who were martyred
For their faith and belief in God above.
So look to the past when you need a reminder
Of how Christianity was born.
It'll make you pause and be thankful
For our religious freedom in this world so torn.

—WEB

Looking Back

Lord, thou hast been our dwelling place in all generations.
Before the mountains were brought forth,
or ever thou hadst formed the earth and the world,
even from everlasting to everlasting, thou art God.

PSALM 90:1–2

The Anabaptist martyrs in Europe were often tortured in
unbelievably hideous ways because of their religious beliefs.
Nevertheless, those early Christians held true to their faith, despite
the horrible things that were done to them. Upon first arriving in
America in the eighteenth century, the Plain People's faith grew and
prospered, despite new and challenging circumstances placed upon
each generation. The Amish keep the martyrs alive in their hearts
even yet today by remembering them through books, such as *The
Martyrs Mirror*, as well as in some of the hymns they sing in their
church *Ausbund* songbook. Hardly a sermon is preached during an
Amish church service without some mention of the Plain People's
forefathers who offered up their lives and accepted death as God's will.

While it's wrong to dwell on the past, it's important for every
believer to remember her or his religious roots. Is there a hymn
or verse of scripture calling you back to remember your spiritual
roots? Open your heart today and let God renew your spirit as you
determine to follow Him for the rest of your days.

Heavenly Father,
thank You for those who've gone before me,
showing by their example what Christianity is about.
Help me to be an example to my friends and family
as I choose to follow You for the rest of my life. Amen.

CHRISTIAN DUTY

We are saved to serve,
but we never serve to get saved.

As we have therefore opportunity, let us do good unto all men, especially unto them who are of the household of faith.

GALATIANS 6:10

Helping Others Is a Christian's Duty

God wants us to help those
Who have special needs.
Giving our time and financial support
Is like planting little seeds.
One person helps another
So no one goes without.
Giving our help and support—
That's what Christianity's about.

—WEB

Financial Support

For where your treasure is, there will your heart be also.
LUKE 12:34

The Amish don't have insurance, so when they get sick or lose a house or a barn, or when someone in the family dies, they must rely on financial support from others. Often this is accomplished through a community benefit auction. My husband and I have attended several benefit auctions, and it's always heartwarming to see the large crowd of Amish who come out in support of others in their community with a financial need.

In our world we hear a lot about ways to become rich so we can provide for our own needs. But the Bible clearly teaches that a Christian's life should not be all about money; it should be about the richness of our relationship with the Lord. It should be about the joy of helping others with a need. Realizing the value of people we care about is more important than all the riches in the world. Acquiring worldly treasures won't bring us happiness, and love is never afraid of giving too much. Is there someone you know who could use some help? Is there a way you or your church can help that person with food, clothing, or financial support?

Heavenly Father,
make my heart sensitive to others in need.
Help me remember that it might be me who has a need
sometime, and remind me to give generously. Amen.

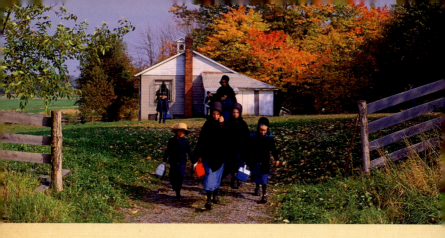

A Duty to Bless Others

So many people are hurting
And need to know that someone cares.
It blesses us as well as them
If we offer encouragement to go with our prayers.
When someone receives a blessing,
They feel a sense of peace;
They know that someone truly cares,
Which helps their worries cease.
It's our Christian duty to bless others—
The Bible tells us so.
For when we edify one another,
The love of Jesus will show.

—WEB

Blessing Others

Wherefore comfort yourselves together,
and edify one another, even as also ye do.

1 THESSALONIANS 5:11

I've seen our Amish friends bless one another many times with their words and deeds. Giving help and comfort during difficult times, encouraging one another not to give up when things look bleak—those are the things that offer a blessing to others.

Our Amish friends have blessed and encouraged my heart as well. One time in particular, when I was struggling with some doubts about my ability to convey to my readers what Amish life is about, one of our Amish friends told me that when she reads my books, she feels as if I am Amish. What a confirmation and a blessing that was to me.

Another time, when I was faced with some personal challenges, one of our Amish friends offered guidance and counsel, assuring me that he and his wife would be praying for my situation.

Life can become overwhelming, but if we take the time to reflect on things, we'll realize that our life is filled with many blessings. Remember the times when you needed a blessing and how uplifted you felt when someone reached out to you in love? Perhaps there's someone you know who needs to receive a blessing today—a touch from God through you.

Heavenly Father,
thank You for those who have blessed my life,
and thank You for the opportunity I have to bless others.
Amen.

The Duty of Community Service

Every Christian has a duty,
To minister to those with a need.
Looking for ways to serve others
Is pleasing to God and doing a good deed.
There are so many opportunities,
To help people throughout our land.
Some folks may have nothing at all;
They need someone to lend a hand.

—WEB

Community Spirit

For God is not unrighteous to forget your work and labour of
love, which ye have shewed toward his name,
in that ye have ministered to the saints, and do minister.

HEBREWS 6:10

The Amish show their community spirit by helping their own whenever there's a need. When a new house or barn is needed, many Amish gather for a time of work, which also results in socializing. We witnessed this several months ago when a new roof was put on one of our Amish friend's homes. The Amish and other Plain communities do many other things that involve them in community service. Some Amish men are volunteer firemen. Some help rebuild homes when devastations like hurricanes and tornadoes occur. Several of our Amish friends went to Louisiana to help rebuild after the destruction caused by hurricane Katrina. Many Amish women make quilts and other items to be sold at various benefit auctions.

Our lives are really about relationships with other people. Perhaps the most important thing we can do as Christians is to help and encourage those who have a need. Look around you. Do you know of someone in your community who has a need? Is there some type of community service you can help with this week?

Heavenly Father,
show me how I can best serve You in ways
that will help others in my community. May Your love
and generosity be shown through me. Amen.

Our Duty to Be Kind

When someone needs some comfort
During their time of need,
Give them the gift of kindness
As you in service lead.
When others offer comfort,
In your time of need,
Accept their gift of kindness,
In every word and deed.

—WEB

Every Good Deed

Look not every man on his own things,
but every man also on the things of others.

PHILIPPIANS 2:4

I remember one day when I was browsing in a store owned by one of our Amish friends. My friend wasn't in the store at the time, but two of her daughters were working there. I'd gone down to the basement of the store and found some secondhand Amish dresses for sale. I picked out two that I particularly liked and took them to one of the young women to ask how much the dresses cost. "Nothing for you," she said with a smile. "Mom would want you to have them."

"Oh, no," I insisted. "I must pay you something for them."

She shook her head, took the dresses, and put them in a paper sack. "Take them, please."

I was tempted to argue further, but I could see by the determined look on her face that she wanted me to have the dresses as a gift. So I smiled and said, "Thank you; I really appreciate this. Tell your mother I said thanks, too."

As I left the store that day, I was struck with the realization that for some people, like me, it's easier to give than to receive. However, we miss many blessings if we don't allow others to give us a gift. When others give to us, we need to be thankful. Believers in Christ have a responsibility to show kindness to others. We also have a responsibility to accept the kindness others show to us.

Heavenly Father,
help me remember not only to show kindness to others,
but to be willing to accept their acts of kindness, too.
Amen.

Our Duty to Attend Church

Whether we attend church in a building

Or gather in someone's house,

We go there to worship and pray.

Whether we travel to church by horse and buggy

Or ride in a fancy, modern car,

We go there to learn about Jesus and how to obey.

The church is God's house,

Where we sing songs of joy.

Where we learn that God loves us—

Every man, woman, girl, and boy.

It's every Christian's duty

To attend the church of their choice,

To hear God's message,

Sing, pray, and rejoice.

—WEB

A True Sense of Worship

Let the word of Christ dwell in you richly in all wisdom;
teaching and admonishing one another in
psalms and hymns and spiritual songs,
singing with grace in your hearts to the Lord.

COLOSSIANS 3:16

The Amish attend church in their home district every other Sunday. On the Sundays they have off from their church, they either visit a church in another district or spend the day reflecting on God's Word and visiting with family and friends.

Since the Amish don't worship in a church building, they have no padded pews to sit on. Instead, they have backless wooden benches. Most English church services don't last more than an hour or so. An Amish church service lasts for three hours, and sometimes longer if young people are being taken into membership. When the service is over, no one rushes out the door, anxious to go home or someplace else. Most everyone stays for the meal and time of fellowship that take place after the service.

When my husband and I attended an Amish church service not long ago, I sensed a worshipful attitude of those in attendance. I heard sincerity in their voices and saw it on their faces.

Think about the last time you attended church. Did you feel a sense of worship? Did you feel God's presence? Did others around you have a worshipful attitude? Memorize this passage of scripture as you worship in God's house this week: "Give unto the Lord the glory due unto his name; worship the Lord in the beauty of holiness" (Psalm 29:2).

Heavenly Father,
thank You for the freedom I have
to worship in Your house each week.
I look forward to being in Your presence
and fellowshipping with other believers. Amen.

Pleasing God Is a Christian's duty

Pleasing God should be our goal;
He sent His Son to save man's soul.
Like a father cares for his young,
God provides for Christians, everyone.
He takes care of those who trust;
The desire to please Him is really a must.

—WEB

Drawing Near to God

Draw nigh to God, and He will draw nigh to you.
JAMES 4:8

One of the most obvious things about the Amish is their desire to yield to God and please Him by the things they say and do. They teach their children to pray before and after each meal. They attend church together and sing songs about God. They give of themselves to others.

While all these things are pleasing to God, what pleases Him more than anything is when we worship Him with our whole heart. This becomes evident when we share the love of God with others through our words and actions.

One thing I've noticed after being with our Amish friends is that for them, God comes first and then their family. It should be every Christian's desire to please God before we please anyone else. Can you think of some things you've done to please God this week? Are there some things you know you ought to do that will please Him, too?

Heavenly Father,
it's my desire to please You in all that I say and do.
Give me the opportunity this week to do
something special that will bring glory to You.
Remind me every day to spend time with You;
for when I'm in Your presence, I feel renewed. Amen.

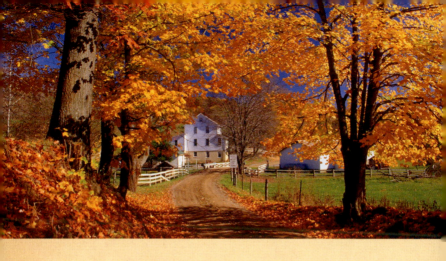

A Christian's Duty to Praise God

I want to remember
To praise God for everything.
No matter if I'm glad or sad,
His praises I will sing.
I want to remember
To worship Him all of my days,
To read God's Holy Bible
And offer my heartfelt praise.

—WEB

Songs of Praise

Serve the LORD with gladness:
come before his presence with singing.

PSALM 100:2

The Amish use no instruments to accompany their singing during church, yet whenever I hear them lift their voices in song, I know they're offering praises to God. Many of the hymns in the Amish *Ausbund*, as well as those hymns found in other denominations' church hymnals, were written to help us understand the beliefs and suffering of those who wrote the hymns of old. These songs are a reminder of the songwriter's faith and were often written during times of suffering, although many of the hymns are songs of praise.

God likes it when we praise Him. In Luke 19:40, Jesus told the Pharisees who had rebuked the people for praising Him that if the people didn't praise Him, the stones would cry out. Songs that glorify God can reach the deepest level of our hearts. What better way for us to praise God than through singing songs of praise?

What are some of your favorite hymns? In what way do the words of the hymns speak to your heart? The next time you sing a hymn, try to visualize the time period it was written and the conditions in which the writer of the hymn lived. Think about the praise it offers to God when you sing the song to Him. Think about the joy it brings to you.

Heavenly Father,
even though my voice is nothing special,
I love singing praises to You.
Thank You for the hymns and choruses
that have been written by others to praise
and worship You. Amen.

A Christian's Duty to Pray

It's more than a duty when I bow my head and pray;

For every sunrise in the east, I thank God for another day.

It's more than a duty when I lift my hands in praise;

When I see stars in the sky, I thank God for all His ways.

It's more than a duty when I get on my knees in prayer;

I ask for a heart of thanksgiving and the willingness to share.

It's more than a duty when I fold my hands in prayer;

I thank God every day for His loving care.

I'm glad I can talk to God any time of the day;

He invites me to do this because He wants me to pray.

I want to pray for others and my own needs, too;

I'm thankful that God loves me and fills my heart anew.

—WEB

Continually Pray

But the prayer of the upright is his delight.
PROVERBS 15:8

The Amish pray before and after each meal and many times throughout the day. They also pray several times during their church services. My husband and I witnessed this firsthand during an Amish wedding and also when we attended an Amish church service. When it was time for prayer, everyone went down on their knees. It wasn't a padded, carpeted floor we knelt on, either. It was a hard, cold cement floor. I found it to be a very humbling experience.

In 1 Thessalonians 5:17, we are told to pray without ceasing. Although some prayers might not be answered in the way we would like, God answers according to His will. We should never quit praying, for there's power in prayer. Each time we pray, our faith will be strengthened. Whenever we pray, God always hears. When we see Him answering our prayers and meeting our needs, our faith will be strengthened and our hearts will be filled with gratitude.

Remember that prayer is nothing more than making your requests known to God. Just as a flower reaches for the sun, we should reach out to God and let His Son bathe our souls.

Heavenly Father,
I thank You for who You are,
and for all that You've done for me.
Help me remember to pray and trust in You,
knowing how much You love and care for me. Amen.

A Christian's Duty to Read God's Word

Sometimes I feel sad and lonely
And think others don't really care;
But when I read my Bible,
I'm reminded that Jesus is always there.
Sometimes I get angry or upset about things.
But when I read God's Word,
My burdens lift and my heart sings.
Sometimes I become frightened by
What's going on in our world today,
But when I read my Bible,
God takes my worries away.

—WEB

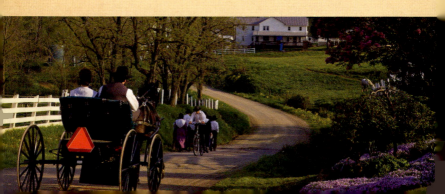

Out of the Darkness

Thy word is a lamp unto my feet,
and a light unto my path.

PSALM 119:105

On one of our visits to Ohio, my husband and I were invited to an auction for a local Amish school. It was still light outside when we arrived, but by the time we left the auction, night had fallen. It was so dark that we couldn't see where our car was parked. "I think we should have brought a flashlight," I told my husband.

Hanging on to each other for support, we took a few tentative steps in the direction of where we'd parked our car. We'd only gone a short ways when a voice from out of the darkness said, "Do you need help finding your car?"

"Yes, we sure do," my husband replied.

"I've got a flashlight, so I'll lead the way." The Amish man who'd spoken pointed a beam of light down the driveway and walked with us to our car. We thanked him for his kindness and were soon on our way.

As we headed down the road, I thought about how unprepared we'd been, going to an event where we knew there'd be no streetlights to guide our way. But the lesson went deeper as I thought about how, when we travel through life, we'll lose our way if we don't have God's Word stamped on our hearts. We need to memorize scripture and never go anywhere in this dark world without it.

Heavenly Father,
fill my heart today with a desire to read, study,
and memorize Your Word. Amen.

Self-Reflection
Is a Christian's Duty

As I spend time in self-reflection,
I'm reminded that, like a pillow for my head,
The love of God supports me.
Like a hungry child needing to be fed,
The Word of God feeds me.
Like a compass showing the way,
The will of God directs me.
Like a warm fire at the end of the day,
The presence of God surrounds me.

—WEB

A Time to Reflect

My meditation of him shall be sweet:
I will be glad in the LORD.

PSALM 104:34

A few years ago, I stood in an Amish schoolhouse in Indiana, watching some children play baseball outside the window. A young Amish boy stepped up to me. "What are you doing?" he asked.

"I'm watching the ball game," I replied.

"You shouldn't be looking out that window."

"Why not?"

His brows puckered. "Because this is the boys' side of the room."

At first, I was a bit put off by the young boy's bold statement. What difference did it make which window, on which side of the room, I'd chosen to look out? After a few minutes of reflection, however, I realized that this was the Amish way, and that as a visitor, I should be respectful and understanding, rather than sensitive to my own needs. I moved over to the girls' side of the entryway, even though there was no ball game going on outside that window.

This incident made me think about the need to do some self-reflection concerning my spiritual life. It's important to spend time in self-reflection every day and ask God if I'm in the place He wants me to be, rather than try to do things my own way. One of the questions I've asked myself this week during my time of meditation is, "Do my actions match the words I speak?" What question do you want to ask God today during your time of self-reflection?

Heavenly Father,
thank you for reminding me that You are faithful, even
when I don't understand Your ways. Help me to appreci-
ate what You provide and remind me that others see my
reactions. I want to be a faithful example for them.
Amen.

Scripture Index

A FINAL THOUGHT

People often judge others by the way they look. God, however, looks at our hearts, not our outward appearance. As believers in Christ, we have the responsibility of caring for the needs of others. The world will see Christ living in us if we set an example by having the right attitude, showing our accountability as followers of Him, and proving by our actions what true Christian service is about. It's my hope that after reading this devotional, you'll not only understand and appreciate the Amish way of life a little better but will find yourself drawing closer to the Lord.

ABOUT THE AUTHOR

WANDA E. BRUNSTETTER enjoys writing about the Amish because they live a peaceful, simple life. Wanda's interest in the Amish and other Plain communities began when she married her husband, Richard, who grew up in a Mennonite church in Pennsylvania. Later, Wanda discovered that her great-great-grandparents were part of the Anabaptist faith. After several years of researching the Amish way of life, Wanda and her husband have developed a close relationship with many Amish families in various communities throughout the United States.

Wanda and her husband have two grown children and six grandchildren. In her spare time, Wanda enjoys photography, ventriloquism, gardening, collecting beach agates and shells, knitting, and having fun with her family.

In addition to numerous stories, articles, poems, and puppet plays, Wanda has written more than fifty books. She and her husband live in Washington State but take every opportunity to visit Amish settlements throughout the country.

Visit Wanda's Web site at www.wandabrunstetter.com and feel free to e-mail her at wanda@wandabrunstetter.com.

OTHER BOOKS BY WANDA E. BRUNSTETTER

FICTION

Lydia's Charm

Indiana Cousins Series
A Cousin's Promise
A Cousin's Prayer
A Cousin's Challenge

Brides of Lehigh Canal Series
Kelly's Chance
Betsy's Return

Sisters of Holmes County Series
A Sister's Secret
A Sister's Test
A Sister's Hope

Brides of Webster County Series
Going Home
On Her Own
Dear to Me
Allison's Journey

(Continued next page)

Daughters of Lancaster County
The Storekeeper's Daughter
The Quilter's Daughter
The Bishop's Daughter

Brides of Lancaster County
A Merry Heart
Looking for a Miracle
Plain and Fancy
The Hope Chest

White Christmas Pie

CHILDREN'S BOOKS

Rachel Yoder—Always Trouble Somewhere Series
School's Out!
Back to School
Out of Control
New Beginnings
A Happy Heart
Just Plain Foolishness
Jumping to Conclusions
Growing Up

The Wisdom of Solomon

NONFICTION

The Simple Life—Devotional Thoughts from Amish Country
Wanda E. Brunstetter's Amish Friends Cookbook
Wanda E. Brunstetter's Amish Friends Cookbook, Vol. 2